AND JESUS Healed THEM All

GLORIA COPELAND

KENNETH
COPELAND
PUBLICATIONS

And Jesus Healed Them All

ISBN-10 1-57562-204-1   30-0518
ISBN-13 978-1-57562-204-0

17 16 15 14 13 12   26 25 24 23 22 21

© 1981 International Church of the Word of Faith Inc. now known as Eagle Mountain International Church aka Kenneth Copeland Publications.

Kenneth Copeland Publications
Fort Worth, TX 76192-0001

For more information about Kenneth Copeland Ministries, visit kcm.org or call 1-800-600-7395 (U.S. only) or +1-817-852-6000.

Contents

Contents

CHAPTER 1

God Wants You Well!

And he came down with them, and stood in the plain, and the company of his disciples, and a great multitude of people out of all Judaea and Jerusalem, and from the sea coast of Tyre and Sidon, which came to hear him, and to be healed of their diseases; and they that were vexed with unclean spirits: and they were healed. And the whole multitude sought to touch him: for there went virtue out of him, and healed them all (Luke 6:17-19).

It is God's will for you to be healed, but your faith cannot operate beyond your knowledge of God's Word. The Word says, "My people are destroyed for lack of knowledge..." (Hosea 4:6). In the physical realm this is literally true. The bodies of born-again believers are being destroyed because they do not have the knowledge of God's Word that it is God's will for them to be healed. Many die young even though it is not God's will. God said, "I will take sickness away from the midst of thee.... The number of thy days I will fulfill" (Exodus 23:25-26). He says in Psalm 91:16, "With long life will I satisfy him, and show him my salvation." It is not the will of God for you to die young. It is God's will for you to live long on the earth without sickness in your midst and to live satisfied!

Healing is not just a New Testament blessing. God has always provided healing for the obedient. Psalm 103:2-3 says, "Bless the Lord, O my soul, and forget not all his benefits: Who forgiveth all thine iniquities; who healeth all thy diseases." Many have forgotten God's benefit of healing for their bodies. If you had been taught that it is God's will to heal you in the same way that you have been taught it is God's will for you to be saved, you would have a different attitude toward sickness. Jesus bore your sicknesses and carried your diseases at the same time and in the same manner that He bore your sins. You are just as free from sickness and disease as you are from sin. You should be as quick to refuse sickness and disease in your body as you are to refuse sin.

Plant the Word

To live free from sickness, you must plant the Word of God concerning healing in your heart. The Bible says that the Word is the incorruptible seed. You are "born again, not of corruptible seed, but of incorruptible, by the word of God, which liveth and abideth for ever" (1 Peter 1:23). You are healed the same way—by the incorruptible seed of the Word of God. *Incorruptible* means that "the seed cannot be destroyed; it cannot be spoiled." Disease cannot stop it. Men cannot spoil that incorruptible seed. Satan cannot stop the power of the Word of God. I can prove that to you with salvation. Once you hear the Word and decide to make Jesus Christ the Lord of your life, there is no power that can stop the new birth from taking place in your spirit. No devil in hell can stop you from being born again. It is the same way with healing. You receive everything from the Lord in the same way—by faith. Results come when you hear the Word, receive it and act on it. You receive healing exactly the way you received the new birth, by hearing the Word and by believing that Word enough to act on it.

You have to put the supernatural seed of the Word of God in your heart. Plant it and it will grow and produce fruit. When you are dealing with God, His time is *now*. He doesn't have to wait 60 days to get a crop. When you plant the Word in your heart, you get the harvest. *Today* is the day of salvation.

Faith should be as highly developed in the Church concerning healing as it is for the new birth of the spirit. If the Church had been told what the Word says about healing, Christians would be as quick to believe that they are healed as they are to believe that they are saved. However, other things have been sown in our hearts. Seeds of doubt and unbelief have been sown by the traditions of men, by men who try to teach the Word with head knowledge instead of by His Spirit.

God's Word doesn't make sense to the carnal mind. Men try to explain the Word through their own natural thinking, but they never succeed. Men in pulpits across our nation have preached things that simply are not true because they have no revelation knowledge of the Word. Traditions cost people the healing power of God. Jesus said the traditions of men make the Word of no effect (Matthew 15:6).

Tradition, Tradition, Tradition

One tradition that has robbed the Church of healing is the practice of praying, "If it be Thy will." You should know that it is God's will to heal you before you ever pray. You can know because God's Word tells you His will. The Word of God is the will of God. "If it be Thy will" is unbelief when praying for healing. There is no faith in that kind of praying. It is the opposite of faith. If you are praying, "Lord, heal me, if it be Thy will," then it is obvious that you don't know what the will of God is, and until you know what God's will is, you don't have any basis for faith. You are like the farmer who sits on his porch and says, "I believe in crops. I know they are real, so I'm not going to plant any seed this year. I'll just believe for my crop to come up." That farmer will sit there forever! It is a principle of life that first you plant, then you reap.

Many Christians today are like that farmer. They are trying to reap a healing harvest when they've not planted any healing seed. "If it be Thy will" will not reap a healing harvest. It will keep you from receiving from God. You can know from God's Word that it is His will for you to be healed.

Another tradition we hear is that healing has passed away. There are no miracles today. God said, "I am the Lord that healeth thee" (Exodus 15:26). We all know that God doesn't change (James 1:17). He has not changed since the beginning of time (Malachi 3:6). For healing to pass away, then God would have to pass away. He is still the Lord that healeth us!

Miracles and the healing power of God are just as available now as when Jesus walked the earth. You can believe that God heals today. Miracles have never passed away—some people just quit believing. It takes active faith to receive from God.

There was a time in my life when I knew that healing was real and that God was healing people, but I didn't know if it was God's will to heal me. Just believing in healing is not enough. You must believe that it is God's will to heal *you*. You have to believe that healing is yours, that it belongs to you. "Healing belongs to me!"

Another tradition tells us that God gets glory from Christians being sick. But the Bible says people gave glory to God when they saw the lame walk and the blind eyes see. People glorified the God of Israel when they saw His power in manifestation (Matthew 15:30-31). Jesus said the Father is glorified when we bear much fruit (John 15:8). Cancer is not fruit. Arthritis is not fruit. The world is not impressed by your sickness. They are not impressed because you bear up under pain and agony. They have all the pain and agony they want. They are looking for a way out of sickness and disease—not a way into it. They have enough problems. They want some answers! People are oppressed by Satan and need deliverance. They want victory in their lives. They want to know how to pay their bills and to be free of sickness in their bodies. That God gets glory from His children being sick makes no sense; but more importantly, it does not agree with the Word.

As believers, we are to be lighthouses of deliverance and help in a dark world. God's will is that we show forth His love and power to the world around us in need of help. The Bible says, "Let your light so shine before men, that they may see your good works, and glorify your Father which is in heaven" (Matthew 5:16).

The world is supposed to see good works in our midst, not sickness and disease. "That ye may be blameless and harmless, the sons of God, without rebuke, in the midst of a crooked and perverse nation, among whom ye shine as lights in the world; holding forth the word of life..." (Philippians 2:15-16). Our commission is to give forth the Word of life—that is the Word of God concerning salvation, healing and deliverance to those around us. Instead, because of the traditions of men, we have tried to tell the world that the God we serve has made us sick. What a lie to tell on the Father God who is the God of love and mercy. Jesus said that we are to lay hands on the sick and they would recover. His will is that His Body be the answer to the problem of sickness and disease. We have been told to alleviate the problem, not teach people that God wants them sick.

Paul's Thorn in the Flesh

One tradition that has been well-taught is referred to as Paul's "thorn in the flesh" from 2 Corinthians 12. (Really it was not Paul's thorn, it was Satan's thorn.) Everyone has heard about it. Tradition teaches that the thorn in the flesh was sickness or disease, but the Word plainly says that the thorn was a "messenger of Satan." This Greek word is translated as *messenger* seven times in the New Testament. It is translated *angel* 181 times in the New Testament.

All 188 times this word is speaking of a personality—not a thing like a sickness or disease. Sickness is not a messenger, nor is it a personality. It was an angel or a messenger of Satan assigned to Paul to buffet him. The word *buffet* means "to give repeated blows, over and over and over." Weymouth's translation says, "Concerning this, three times have I besought the Lord that he might leave me" (2 Corinthians 12:8). The *King James Version* says, "For this thing I besought the Lord thrice, that it might depart from me." The thorn in the flesh was not a sickness as tradition teaches, but a messenger from Satan as the Bible teaches. God does not use Satan's messenger service. God did not give Paul this thorn in the flesh—Satan sent Paul the thorn to stop the Word from being preached.

We see an example where Satan buffeted Paul:

But when the Jews saw the multitudes, they were filled with envy, and spake against those things which were spoken by Paul, contradicting and blaspheming.... But the Jews stirred up the devout and honourable women, and the chief men of the city, and raised persecution against Paul and Barnabas, and expelled them out of their coasts.... When there was an assault made both of the Gentiles, and also of the Jews with their rulers, to use them despitefully, and to stone them, they were ware of it, and fled unto Lystra.... And there came thither certain Jews from Antioch and Iconium, who persuaded the people, and, having stoned Paul, drew him out of the city, supposing he had been dead. Howbeit, as the disciples stood round about him, he rose up, and came into the city: and the next day he departed with Barnabas to Derbe (Acts 13:45, 50, 14:5-6, 19-20).

In every place, the messenger of Satan stirred up persecution and affliction against Paul—blow after blow, buffet after buffet. Everywhere he went, there was trouble and persecution.

The terms thorn in the flesh or "thorn in the side" are always used as an illustration in the Bible. For example, the Lord told Moses that if the Israelites did not drive out the inhabitants of the land of Canaan, they would become "pricks in [their] eyes, and thorns in [their] sides..." (Numbers 33:55). The Canaanites were not sticking into the Israelites' sides! This is just an illustration. Today, we still use the term "a thorn in the

flesh." Your neighbor might be a "thorn" in your
side. In the same way we say, "That guy is a pain
in the neck." Tradition says this thorn in the flesh
was something in Paul's flesh, but 2 Corinthians
12:7 is the same type of illustration. Weymouth's
translation of this verse says, "There was given
me a thorn in the flesh, *Satan's angel* to torture
me." This evil spirit was assigned to Paul in order
to stop the Word. Jesus said in Mark 4 that Satan
comes immediately to steal the Word. Paul was
having to stand against this evil spirit everywhere
he went.

Satan came to buffet Paul because of the abundance of revelations he received. Paul had been
given the revelation of the authority of the be--
liever, and Satan came to steal the Word. Paul
sought the Lord three times that he might be
rid of him. It is useless to ask God to get rid of
the devil for you. Paul had authority over Satan.
It was up to him to use that authority. The Bible
says, "...Resist the devil, and he will flee from
you" (James 4:7). God won't resist the devil for
you. You have to do it. If you don't cast out the
devil, you will just have to live with him or get
somebody else to help you get rid of him.

When Paul asked God to do something about
this messenger of Satan, the Lord said, "My grace
is sufficient for thee..." (2 Corinthians 12:9).
Tradition reads that as if he asked the Lord to

deliver him and the Lord said no. Therefore, Paul had to endure the thorn forever. The Bible actually says, "And he said unto me, My grace is sufficient for thee: for my strength is made perfect in weakness." God was saying, "My favor is enough. You have authority. You have the Name of Jesus and when you're humanly weak, My strength or My power is made perfect."

We can see an excellent example of this in Acts 14, when Paul was stoned. He was dead, but the disciples gathered around him, prayed and the Lord raised him up. It was humanly impossible for him to do anything. In his own strength he had no ability to overcome. But when he was humanly weak, the power of God was strong.

In 2 Corinthians 12:10, Paul wrote, "Therefore I take pleasure in infirmities, in reproaches, in necessities, in persecutions, in distresses for Christ's sake...." Let's look over these words. *Infirmity* means "want of strength, weakness, indicating inability to produce results." It does not mean sickness. It means what the Lord said: "When your strength ends, My power is made perfect." The other things mentioned here—reproaches, necessities, persecutions, distresses—are the buffetings Paul lists in 2 Corinthians 11. He was imprisoned, stoned, beaten, shipwrecked and attacked by angry mobs. Sickness is not mentioned.

We have heard a lot about trials and tribulations that came on Paul, but tradition forgets to mention that Satan's angel could gain no victory over Paul through adverse circumstances. Paul lived to be an old man. When it was time for him to go, he said he didn't know whether he wanted to stay or depart (Philippians 1:20-26). Paul did not go home to be with the Lord until he and the Lord were ready. He was a victorious Christian. He wrote most of the New Testament. He traveled throughout the known world. Satan's angel never could stop the Word of God from going forth.

Paul's own testimony was, "For I am now ready to be offered, and the time of my departure is at hand. I have fought a good fight, I have finished my course, I have kept the faith" (2 Timothy 4:6-7). That is not a description of a man who was sick or weak. Glory to God!

When you are sick, you don't do very much. You are not strong. You stay right where you are and worry about your own body. When you are sick, you're not thinking about laying hands on someone else to get them healed. Paul couldn't have finished the course had he been a sick man. He couldn't fight a good fight and be sick. The fight of faith is a good fight because it's a fight you win.

It is my desire to make this same statement when it is time for me to depart. "I have fought a good fight. I have finished the course. I have kept the faith." To me, those are strong, victorious words. Just think about that. This man was strong in the Lord!

In Philippians 4:12-13, *The Amplified Bible*, Paul said, "I have learned in any and all circumstances the secret of facing every situation...I have strength for all things in Christ Who empowers me [I am ready for anything and equal to anything through Him Who infuses inner strength into me." Paul learned to rely on the One within him to put him over. He quit trying to do things by himself. He knew he was strong in the Lord, not in his own might.

In Acts 9:16 the Lord said, "I will show him [Paul] how great things he must suffer for my name's sake." Paul knew he would undergo persecutions and afflictions, and he agreed to it. He wanted to do the will of God at any cost.

Paul was a victorious man. He said, "Persecutions, sufferings, such as occurred to me at Antioch, at Iconium, and at Lystra, persecutions I endured, but out of them all the Lord delivered me" (2 Timothy 3:11, *The Amplified Bible)*. Tradition forgets to tell us that! Paul faced trials and tribulations, but the Lord delivered him out of them all! The thorn in the flesh that we have heard so much about could gain no victory over Paul and the Word of God. The messenger of Satan could only aggravate and harass him. He could not stop the Word from going forth. There is a big difference in being aggravated and being defeated! In every situation Paul faced, even death by stoning, the power of God was made strong and delivered him.

We hear so much more about the thorn in the flesh than about the outcome. Paul was delivered from every opposition, from every evil work. When human strength ends, the power of God excels. This is what we should have been taught about the thorn in the flesh. This is teaching that the Church needs to hear: When human strength ends, the power of God excels!

You can see how helpless we have been with traditions planted in our hearts and minds instead of God's Word. You cannot stand in faith against sickness and disease when you have been taught that sickness is God's will for you. How can you stand in faith when you think God has put cancer on you to teach you something? This tradition is an abomination to the nature of God! How can you say that a loving God would put sickness on you to teach you something? If you believe that, then you need to quit taking your medicine. If it is God's will for you to be sick, then to take medicine would be to fight against the will of God.

Your Power of Authority

Some people accept sickness as God's will. Yet the same people will take medicine, be operated on, or do anything else they can in order to get well. Christianity is not just on Sunday morning. Spiritual things work every day of the week. The Bible makes sense because it works! It works on Monday just like it does on Sunday. It is God's wisdom written in man's words, so that we can be victorious on the earth.

Some people say, "Well, maybe God doesn't put sickness on you, but He allows Satan to." There is only one person who allows Satan to put sickness on you, and that is you.

As a believer, you have authority in the earth over Satan and sickness and disease. If sickness has come upon you, you have allowed it, not God. God doesn't have to allow Satan to make you sick. Satan is always ready to do the job! Sickness incapacitates you and makes you no threat to Satan at all.

You need to lay aside what tradition has taught you and realize that only Satan could be the source of such powerless, defeated beliefs. The Word of God is the incorruptible seed. Satan does not have the power to stop it. Disease cannot overcome it. Only you have the power to stop the Word from working in your life.

As you study the incorruptible seed of the Word of God, keep your mind and spirit open to the Word to change your thinking. Doubt and unbelief will come against you and say, "Now, you know what they say about this...." Who are "they"? Well, "they" will be the ones who bury you early if you listen to their traditions. Cast out the doubt and keep the Word.

Receive the Word. The power and blessing that you get out of the Word of God is according to how you receive it. You must receive it literally as God talking to you, as the Word of God and the authority in your life. You must decide that whatever you see in the Word you will act on. If you just receive it a little here and a little there, thinking, *Well, now, that could be true,* you will get nothing from the Word. You have to receive the Word and give it the place of authority in your life. When you allow the incorruptible seed to go into your heart, it will produce the crop you desire.

CHAPTER 2

God's Medicine

Proverbs 4:20-21 describes God's prescription for life and health. If you are well, it will keep you well. If you are sick, it will heal you and then keep you well. There has never been a miracle drug that could equal the Word of God. God's medicine is the answer to every need.

This is the way the power of God works through the Word. If you put the Word of God in your heart, act on it and obey it, you will always get healed. Take the time to put the Word in your heart concerning healing and keep that Word alive, and the power and the faith of God will always be ready to minister to you as you release your faith. The power of God is always there for the believer who will take the time to put God's Word in his heart.

Healing is always available to the believer, but faith has to be released in order for you to receive the healing power of God. If you have been feeding your spirit with the Word as you are supposed to, then the moment a symptom of sickness comes against your body, your faith is there to rise up within you and put power behind your words.

If you are a new believer and haven't had the time to put the Word in your heart, you need help and there are people to help you. You can have hands laid on you. But don't stay in an elementary condition. Develop your own faith. Don't allow the storms of life to overtake you. Get in the Word and renew your mind. Begin to think like God thinks and you will act like God acts. Proverbs 4:20-23 says: "My son, attend to my words; incline thine ear unto my sayings. Let them not depart from thine eyes; keep them in the midst of thine heart. For they are life unto those that find them, and health to all their flesh. Keep thy heart with all diligence; for out of it are the issues of life."

God's prescription is for life and health. God says His words are life to all that find them and health to all their flesh. This means that cancer has to go, arthritis has to go, sickness and disease have to go. The Word of God is health to all your flesh; but to enjoy the benefits of the Word, you have to do what the Word says.

If you have a terminal disease and the doctor has said you have only a short time to live, God's

Word will be life to you. The Word will prolong your life and cause you to fulfill your days on the earth (Exodus 23:26). It is the life of God. God's Word is life to those who find it! But what about those who don't find it? They are not mentioned here because the ones who don't find it are the ones who perish for a lack of knowledge. Those who do find it are the ones who are healed and live long on the earth.

Attend to My Words

"Attend to my words." Give your undivided attention to God's Word. Pay heed to what He says. Whatever it says, you believe it and act on it. If you attend to someone, you take care of that person. There is still only one thing that is needful and that is the Word of God. It is the one thing that a believer cannot successfully do without. If you will attend to the Word and spend time in it, every other situation in your life will be taken care of because of the faith, knowledge and wisdom that come from God's Word. Everything we do should revolve around the Word of God because it has the answer to every problem. The Word of God will make your time count. It will save you mistakes that cost time. Sickness costs time. The Word of God will make your life better and your time more productive. You cannot afford to be without the Word.

Whenever I get under pressure and begin to think, *There's no way that I can do all that I've got to do,* I know immediately that I have not been spending enough time in God's Word. When I get bogged down in the affairs of life and pressure comes, I know that my time in the Word has gone for something else. The Word of God causes your life to work. You won't get bogged down in the affairs of life if you will spend time in the Word, to meditate in it and see what God is saying to you.

The Bible says, "Thou wilt keep him in perfect peace, whose mind is stayed on thee: because he trusteth in thee" (Isaiah 26:3). When you spend time in the Word and stay your mind on it, you will be kept in perfect peace and you will trust in Him. That is faith. Romans 10:17 says faith comes by hearing and hearing by the Word of God. You will be kept in this perfect peace because you trust in Him. Your faith will stay strong and you will be trusting in the Lord, not in the things you can see.

When you keep your attention on God's Word, your mind will be free from doubt. Many people try to believe, but don't have the Word in their hearts. Faith is not a mental process. Believing in the heart comes from time spent in the Word of God. It takes more than just a mental decision to cause your vocabulary to be in line with God's Word.

Jesus said, "Out of the abundance of the heart the mouth speaketh" (Matthew 12:34). You have to get God's Word into your heart in abundance so that it has more reality to you than the things you see. In other words, if you're sick, you need to come to a place where the Word of God has so much reality to you that the symptoms in your body count for nothing. That's what Abraham did. He was fully persuaded that God was able and mighty to keep His Word (Romans 4:21). It didn't matter to him that he was 100 years old and that the time for Sarah to bear children had passed. He didn't look at that. He was fully persuaded that the Word of God was true.

You have to put the Word of God in your heart until the reality of your healing has more power and validity to you than the symptoms of sickness coming on your body. That revelation will only come from attending to God's Word—keeping yourself in the Word of God and putting it in your heart in abundance. You can come to the place where the Word of God has more authority than what you can see or feel. If you see or feel something that is opposite from the Word, you'll not be moved by it because you are moved only by God's Word.

Incline Thine Ear Unto My Sayings

"Incline thine ear unto my sayings." Desire and go after God's Word. Put your ear in position to hear the word of faith preached. Don't wait for someone to come to your town. Go to where the

Word is being preached. Believers are moving from one city to another because they want to get under the Word and receive what God has for them. They are going to any lengths to get under the Word. They know that if they get the Word in their hearts, they can get anything else they need. If you spend enough time in the Word, it will change everything you do.

Jesus said: "If any man has ears to hear, let him be listening and let him perceive and comprehend. And He said to them, Be careful what you are hearing. The measure [of thought and study] you give [to the truth you hear] will be the measure [of virtue and knowledge] that comes back to you—and more [besides] will be given to you who hear (Mark 4:23-24, *The Amplified Bible).*

We measure to ourselves the blessing of the Lord by the attention, respect and heed we give to His Word. If you give just a little heed to it, that's all you are going to receive. If you give total heed and attention to God's Word, the power that comes back to you will be great and it will produce results in your life.

Jesus said to be careful how you hear. Don't hear through tradition. Don't make the Word of God sift its way through traditional ears. It won't work for you. Receive God's Word willingly. Allow it to be unhindered by anything you have ever known or experienced.

To prosper in the faith walk, you must first make a decision that God's Word does not fail. If the Word of God does not seem to be working for you, it's not God's fault. There is something you don't know. More than likely, you are just not standing firm. The Bible says, "And having done all, to stand. Stand therefore..." (Ephesians 6:13-14). It says, "Stand." That's all. It doesn't say for how long. If you catch yourself saying, "Well, the Word is not working for me," then you can know automatically that you are not standing. You must have a steadfast faith when it comes to God's Word. If it is not steadfast, it is not faith. One thing you must know is: *God's Word does not fail!*

These things work for the obedient. When God said, "I am the Lord that healeth thee," He said that they were to serve Him. When He said, "I will take sickness away from the midst of thee," He also said, "if you will serve Me." In other places He says, "If you are diligent to do My Word...." There are things we can do in order to be in line with the healing power of God. Make the decision to know that failure is not on God's behalf. It is not a failure of His Word. God doesn't make mistakes, but His children do. When Satan tries to make you mad at God and you say, "God, I've done all these things. I've confessed Your Word and it's not working for me," you can remember that it is not God. God never fails. The Word never fails. Don't test and examine God. Test and examine yourself. Don't judge God. Judge yourself.

"Let them not depart from thine eyes." Keep your eyes trained on the Word of God. Don't look at the circumstances that appear contrary to what you are believing for. Keep your eyes on the Word of God. Be like Abraham and consider the Word instead of your body. What you receive through your eyes and ears can make the difference between life and death, so keep the Word before your eyes and keep the Word going in your ears. What you believe in your heart is regulated by what you give your attention to.

Keep Them in the Midst of Thine Heart

"Keep them in the midst of thine heart." Keep the Word of God alive in your heart. Keep the Word working in your heart. Just as you feed your physical man, you must feed your spiritual man. Your spirit man cannot live and stay strong on the Word you received last year. Don't try to rely on what you remember from the Word. Keep God's words in the midst of your heart by doing the things we have already discussed: attending to the Word, inclining your ear to the Word, not letting the Word depart from your eyes and keeping the Word in your heart. Keep your spirit strong with the Word of God. Continually feed yourself with it in order to keep the Word producing the force of faith.

For They Are Life Unto Those That Find Them and Health to All Their Flesh

"For they are life unto those that find them, and health to all their flesh." God's words are spirit and they are life (John 6:63). They are made life and health to those who find them. The Word of God is medicine. If you will put it in your heart in abundance, it will be as hard for you to get sick as it was at one time for you to get healed. (The key to this statement is in the word *abundance!)* God's prescription for life and health works constantly, whether you are sick or well. The Word is continually being made life and health to your body. Satan cannot make you sick when you stay strong in the Word and keep your spirit full of God's Word. By keeping the Word in the midst of your heart, the healing power of God will continually work in your body. It is continually being made health to your flesh.

When the doctor prescribes medication, he tells you to take the medicine so many times a day and you will recover. If the doctor says swallow one teaspoon of this every day and you decide to rub it on your chest, all of his knowledge and experience is of no value. If you expect to be well, you follow his instructions, don't you? Well, this is *God's* prescription. His Word is His medicine. If you will do what He says as diligently as you would obey a doctor, you will get results.

Diligence in the Word of God is a key. When your doctor says you need surgery, you don't say, "Well, Doc, I don't have time to have an operation." No, you make time, even if you lose your job. Be that courageous, diligent and determined about the Word of God. Make time to attend to God's Word. It will bring far better results!

Keep Thy Heart With All Diligence

"Keep thy heart with all diligence." Be diligent about keeping God's Word in your heart. Continually attending to it with your ears, your eyes and your heart will cause you to live in divine health. The Word of God will continually be made life and health to your body. Don't attend to the sickness. Attend to God's Word. Whether you are sick or well, the Word is continually made life and health to your flesh. This is the surest way to stay healed. To be sick and then receive healing is not God's best. God's best is for you to live in divine health, to have divine life continually flowing from your spirit man to your physical man— keeping your physical body well. "But if the Spirit of him that raised up Jesus from the dead dwell in you, he that raised up Christ from the dead shall also quicken your mortal bodies by his Spirit that dwelleth in you" (Romans 8:11).

"Keep thy heart with all diligence; for out of it are the issues of life." The forces of life bring healing power. Out of your heart comes the force of faith to relieve you of any problem that Satan would try to bring on you. God's best is for you to keep your heart with all diligence and have the forces of life continually coming out of your spirit. This realm of God's very best is available to every one of us if we will spend time in the Word. The forces of life and power coming from the heart are in direct proportion to the amount of Word going in us and the attention or heed we give it. There is no limit to the amount of God's medicine that you can take. You cannot get an overdose. The more you take, the stronger you get.

Speaking Faith

Mark 11:23-24 says: "For verily I say unto you, That whosoever shall say unto this mountain, Be thou removed, and be thou cast into the sea; and shall not doubt in his heart, but shall believe that those things which he saith shall come to pass; he shall have whatsoever he saith. Therefore I say unto you, What things soever ye desire, when ye pray, believe that ye receive them, and ye shall have them."

The things you speak consistently are what will come to pass in your life. What you continually say with your mouth is what you believe in your heart. Your words are your faith speaking. If there is a mountain in your way, don't ask God to do something about it. You speak to it. You speak to the sickness or disease. You speak to the symptom coming at your body: "Pain, I speak to you in the Name of Jesus and I command you to leave my body. Arthritis, I speak to you in Jesus' Name and I command you to leave my body."

When you pray is when you believe you receive. Believe you receive your healing when you pray, not when you feel better. This is how faith works. You receive, not according to how much better or worse you feel, but according to what the Word says. Accept the Word and don't go back on it. Give your attention to God's Word, not the symptoms of sickness or disease. Make up your mind to stand, no matter how long it takes. Determine to be steadfast in the faith.

If the symptoms of sickness or disease continue to linger, this is the time that you must hold fast to a fearless confession of the Word of God. Hebrews 10:35-36 in *The Amplified Bible* says: "Do not, therefore, fling away your fearless confidence, for it carries a great and glorious compensation of reward. For you have need of steadfast patience and endurance, so that you may perform and fully accomplish the will of God, and thus receive and carry away [and enjoy to the full] what is promised."

It is so important that you learn to be steadfast. Once you learn to be steadfast in your faith concerning healing, you will know how to be steadfast in other areas. When you learn to be moved by God's Word—not by circumstances, not by how you feel or what you see—you can receive anything that God's Word offers. Healing is a good place for you to learn steadfastness. When you can be steadfast on the Word of God with pain in your body, then you can certainly be steadfast on the Word of God with your bank account or anything else. When you stand steadfast until you receive the answer, you will always get results.

Do not waver. Abraham did not waver. No unbelief or distrust made him waver. Doubt will keep you out of the blessings of God. Wavering is doubt. Train yourself to rely only on what God's Word says. Train your eyes and your ears to be obedient to the Word. What your eye sees does not discount the Word of God. What your ear hears does not discount the Word of God. Bad news does not discount the Word of God. Your heart is established, trusting in the Lord. The thing that should be in authority in you is the Word of God. Go by what God's Word says. It is the key to victory in any situation. Learn to rely on God's Word.

There were 19 different cases of Jesus healing individuals in the New Testament. In 12 out of the 19, the scriptures refer to the individual's faith. For instance, to the woman with the issue of blood Jesus said, "Thy faith hath made thee whole" (Mark 5:34). She drew on that healing power and Jesus knew when it left Him. Your faith is important when you are being prayed for. You come to receive healing in your body, not just to have hands laid on you. Your faith is what draws the power of God into your body or circumstances. You receive according to your faith. Faith activates the power of God. Faith activates the healing power of God in your body. Faith gives action to healing power. When you say, "I believe I receive healing for my body from the top of my head to the soles of my feet," you are activating the healing power of God. The woman with the issue of blood said, "If I may touch but his clothes, I shall be whole" (Mark 5:28). She said it, she did it and she received it.

Expect to Receive

All you have to do is expect to receive. It's what you do with your faith. *Expect* God's Word to bring healing into your body. Expect God to be true to His Word. Galatians 3:5 says, "He therefore that ministereth to you the Spirit, and worketh miracles among you, doeth he it by the works of the law, or by the hearing of faith?" Miracles are wrought by faith.

The Word will open your heart to receive. Unbelief kept Jesus from doing mighty works in Nazareth. The Bible says He marveled at their unbelief (Mark 6:6). The Word will rid you of unbelief. It will rid you of bad teaching that robs you of God's power. Receive the Word and stand in faith. Demand that doubt and unbelief go somewhere else.

In Acts 4:24-30, believers prayed in one accord and asked the Lord to stretch forth His hand to heal and to perform signs and wonders. Then in the next chapter, it says the multitudes brought their sick and "they were healed every one" (Acts 5:12-16). This is a demonstration of corporate faith. They were working together, believing for a manifestation of the healing power of God.

We need to stretch out the borders of our faith in the Body of Christ to believe that *every* sick person who comes in our midst will receive the healing power of God. That is what God wants. It is His will. We can see it in the earthly ministry of Jesus.

CHAPTER 3

Jesus Healed Them All

"Philip saith unto him, Lord, show us the Father, and it sufficeth us. Jesus saith unto him...he that hath seen me hath seen the Father.... Believest thou not that I am in the Father, and the Father in me? the words that I speak unto you I speak not of myself: but the Father that dwelleth in me, he doeth the works" (John 14:8-10).

If you want to see the Father, look at Jesus. During His ministry on earth, Jesus revealed to men the express will of God in action. When you have seen Jesus, you have seen the Father.

Jesus did not even speak His own words. He spoke the Father's words. He did not take credit for the works done in His ministry but said that the Father in Him did the works.

Everything that He said and did was a picture

of the Father's will. Jesus said in John 8:28, *The Amplified Bible*, "I do nothing of Myself (of My own accord or on My own authority), but I say [exactly] what My Father has taught Me." He was God's vehicle on the earth, God's way to man and man's way to God. "For I came down from heaven, not to do mine own will, but the will of him that sent me" (John 6:38). First John 3:8 says, "For this purpose the Son of God was manifested, that he might destroy the works of the devil." Jesus came to do God's will in the earth. His will was for Jesus to destroy the works of the devil. God set Jesus in direct opposition to Satan, the curse and all its evil effects.

Every move that Jesus made and every word that He said was geared to destroy the work of Satan. Every work of power and every healing was the will of God.

If you believe God's Word, you have to believe that Jesus' attitude toward sickness is God's attitude toward sickness.

He Healed All—Every—Any

Watch God's will concerning healing in the ministry of Jesus. Watch for the words *all, every* and *any*. "But when Jesus knew it, he withdrew himself from thence: and great multitudes followed him, and he healed them all" (Matthew 12:15). Even in a great multitude of people,

Jesus healed them all. This means that not one was left sick!

"And Jesus went forth, and saw a great multitude, and was moved with compassion toward them, and he healed their sick" (Matthew 14:14). Not just some of their sick—all of them.

Matthew 15:30-31 says: "And great multitudes came unto him, having with them those that were lame, blind, dumb, maimed, and many others, and cast them down at Jesus' feet; and he healed them: Insomuch that the multitude wondered, when they saw the dumb to speak, the maimed to be whole, the lame to walk, and the blind to see: and they glorified the God of Israel." (Notice when God gets glory!)

Luke 4:40 says: "Now when the sun was setting, all they that had any sick with divers diseases brought them unto him; and he laid his hands on every one of them, and healed them." Any who were sick were brought to Him. He laid His hands on every one of them and healed them.

Luke 6:17-19 says:

And he came down with them, and stood in the plain, and the company of his disciples, and a great multitude of people out of all Judaea and Jerusalem, and from the sea coast of Tyre and Sidon, which came to hear him, and to be healed of their diseases; and they that were vexed with unclean spirits: and they were healed. And the whole multitude sought to touch him: for there went virtue out of him, and healed them all.

The multitude came to hear Jesus, but they also came to be healed. They came expecting to receive. They knew that if they could get where Jesus was, they would receive healing. They came to be healed! He healed them *all.* Not even in a great multitude was there a person that Jesus would not heal. You know that in a great multitude there were all kinds of people—good and bad, but Jesus healed them all. If there was anything that could disqualify one from receiving healing, surely in a great multitude you would find one who was so bad that he could not receive. Jesus healed them all! Thank God the Bible tells us in Hebrews 13:8 that He is the same yesterday, today and forever.

Luke 13:10-11 says:

And he was teaching in one of the syna-gogues on the sabbath. And, behold, there was a woman which had a spirit of in--firmity eighteen years, and was bowed together, and could in no wise lift up her-self. And when Jesus saw her, he called her to him, and said unto her, Woman, thou art loosed from thine infirmity. And he laid his hands on her: and immediately she was made straight, and glorified God. And the ruler of the synagogue answered with indignation, because that Jesus had healed on the sabbath day, and said unto the people, There are six days in which men ought to work: in them therefore come and be healed, and not on the sabbath day. The Lord then answered him, and said, Thou hypocrite, doth not each one of you on the sabbath loose his ox or his ass from the stall, and lead him away to watering? And ought not this woman, being a daughter of Abraham, whom Satan hath bound, lo, these eighteen years, be loosed from this bond on the sabbath day?

Jesus said Satan had bound this woman. She was a daughter of Abraham and had a covenant with God. She had faith to be healed because Jesus was teaching and preaching about the covenant. He was telling the people what belonged to them. He was telling them that the Spirit of the Lord was upon Him and that He was anointed to preach the gospel and release the captives. Because of His words, they were able to receive. This woman had a covenant.

She had a right to be healed! She was a daughter of Abraham and should have been loosed, yet Satan had kept her bound for 18 years! Jesus commanded Satan to loose her and she was made straight.

We are in the same position today. We have a covenant with God and Jesus has already paid the price for our sicknesses and our diseases. Every one of us should be loosed from the bondage of Satan. We have the same authority to do just what Jesus did—to command sickness and disease to depart. He said, "Woman, thou art loosed from thine infirmity" (Luke 13:12). He executed judgment in that situation, and she was loosed from the bondage of Satan. This is a picture of the Church executing judgment in the earth. When you lay hands on the sick, you are executing judgment—declaring that the prince of this world (Satan) has been judged and that the power of sickness and disease has been destroyed (John 16:11). The authority in the Name of Jesus belongs to you because you are a believer. In His Name you are taking authority over sickness and disease in another person's body and commanding it to leave. It will go! The Word says if you resist the devil, he will flee from you (James 4:7). As God's representative, you can cast out devils. You can lay hands on the sick and they shall recover.

Let Go of Doubt

Look at Acts 10:38 and see how Peter describes Jesus' ministry after three years of close association with Him: "How God anointed Jesus of Nazareth with the Holy Ghost and with power: who went about doing good, and healing all that were oppressed of the devil; for God was with him." Did He just heal some? No. He healed all who were oppressed of the devil.

The only record of anything hindering Jesus from accomplishing the will of God in the lives of His people occurred in Nazareth. It was not God's will that stopped His miracle and healing power; it was the will of the people there. He could do no mighty works because of their unbelief (Mark 6:5-6). Doubt will rob you of God's blessings. Unbelief will rob you and leave you sick. There is only one thing that can stop doubt and unbelief in the heart of a man and that is the Word of God. When a person receives the Word, doubt, defeat and discouragement have to leave. Don't hang on to any doubt or unbelief. Don't even dwell on it. Let the Word of God expel it.

I absolutely refuse to feed my spirit on doubt and unbelief because I know that my very life depends on the faith of God in my spirit. I will not sit under any teacher or preacher who puts doubt and unbelief in my spirit. What you feed into your spirit is a matter of life and death, a matter of victory and defeat. Faith comes by hearing the Word of God. Doubt comes by hearing unbelief. It is important what you hear.

The Scriptures show beyond doubt that Jesus, while fulfilling the will of God, offered healing unconditionally during His ministry in the earth. God has never been stingy with His healing power. He has always desired that you be healed. He wants you to be healed even more than you do. Because of His great compassion and love for His family, God greatly desires to manifest His power in our midst, yet He works only by faith—no other way.

God's Desire for You

As a parent, when you see your child sick or unhappy or hurting, you would give anything to get deliverance for him. Your heart yearns for that. God is the same way with His children. He yearns for you to receive His power freely, for you to release faith and believe His compassionate nature. Believe His Word, believe His healing power so He can lavish it upon you. Get in the Word and find out what God's Word says about you. Find out what His will is, then open your spirit to receive the power of God. Let the power of God flow through you unhindered, in the Name of Jesus. We all want the power of God working in our lives and we can have it. It is available to us. We need to set our goal to be the ones through whom the power of God can flow. When we believe God's Word, put it first place and do whatever it says to do, doubt, tradition and unbelief cannot hold us back.

It should be the goal of every believer to be a vessel God can use—a vessel unto honor, fit and ready for any good work (2 Timothy 2:21, *The Amplified Bible)*. God is wanting vessels that He can use—not vessels tied down by the traditions of men and the things of the world. He wants men and women through whom He can work freely. To be those vessels unto honor requires our decision to cooperate with God's Word, to get in line with it and purge ourselves from the things that would rob us of the power of God. For example, we are to walk in love and keep the commandment of God. The commandment of the Church is 1 John 3:22, "And whatsoever we ask, we receive of him, because we keep his commandments, and do those things that are pleasing in his sight." Not walking in love will rob us of the power of God. A firm determination to walk in love will permit His power to flow through us freely.

We have seen the availability of God's power during the earthly ministry of Jesus. Healing was offered to whomever would receive Him and believe His words. Now let's look at the book of Acts and see what the Church's attitude toward sickness and disease was: "There came also a multitude out of the cities round about unto Jerusalem, bringing sick folks, and them which were vexed with unclean spirits: and they were healed every one" (Acts 5:16).

When Jesus was on the earth, healing power moved through His body to effect a healing and a cure. The people sought to touch Him. After He sat down at the right hand of the Father, healing power still moved through His Body, the Church, to heal all! Multitudes came out to get healed. They brought their sick for one reason: because they expected to receive. And they did receive! They were healed every one.

The healing power of God flowed! You need to get that in your spirit. It flowed!

Years later, Paul was shipwrecked on an island. He didn't plan to be there; he had every intention of passing it by. He had not planned a great healing campaign on Melita. Was healing power still offered unconditionally?

Look at Acts 28:8-9: "And it came to pass, that the father of Publius lay sick of a fever and of a bloody flux: to whom Paul entered in, and prayed, and laid his hands on him, and healed him. So when this was done, others also, which had diseases in the island, came, and were healed."

Weymouth's translation says, all the other sick people on the island came to get healed and they were healed. God's power is not exclusive. This was not a planned campaign; but Paul was there, so he laid hands on the sick and they received. They all got healed!

James 5:14-15 says if you have any sick among you, call on the elders of the church and let them pray over them, anointing them with oil; and the prayer of faith shall save the sick—not just some sick, any sick.

It is against the will of God for you to be sick. From the beginning of time the Word of God has offered God's healing power to any who would be obedient and come to receive. There was not a multitude so large that even one remained sick. Jesus healed them all! The leper said, "If You will, You can make me clean." Jesus said, "I will" (Mark 1:40-41). You will never see Jesus refusing to heal anyone. You will never hear Him say, "You're going to have to keep the sickness two more weeks because the Father and I are trying to teach you something." You will never hear that! You will never hear Jesus saying, "You'll have to remain blind because we want people to give glory to God." Jesus never withheld the healing power of God, not even in Nazareth. It was their will—their unwillingness to receive—that kept them from receiving. God's will never changed.

CHAPTER 4

He Bore Our Sicknesses

"That it might be fulfilled which was spoken by Esaias the prophet, saying, Himself took our infirmities, and bare our sicknesses" (Matthew 8:17).

When Jesus bore away our sins, He also bore away our diseases. The Cross pronounced a complete cure for the ills of mankind.

The Church of Jesus Christ has been made just as free from sickness as it has been made free from sin. A Christian may continue to sin after he has been born again, but he does not have to. Sin shall no longer lord it over him unless he allows it (Romans 6:14).

A Christian may continue to be sick after he has been born again, but he does not have to. He has been redeemed from sickness. The price has been paid for his healing. Sickness can no longer exert dominion over him unless he allows it.

Most believers have only known a part of their

redemption. Their faith will operate to the degree of their knowledge of God's Word. They would have begun to live in divine health long ago if they had realized that healing belonged to them.

As you accept the fact that as surely as Jesus bore your sins, He also bore away your disease, weakness and pain, your days of sickness will be over.

The light of the Word of God will destroy Satan's grip in your life in the area of physical suffering. The truth makes you free from his dominion when you realize that your healing has already been purchased by the sacrifice of Jesus. Isaiah 53:4-5 says, "Surely he hath borne our griefs, and carried our sorrows: yet we did esteem him stricken, smitten of God, and afflicted. But he was wounded for our transgressions, he was bruised for our iniquities: the chastisement of our peace was upon him; and with his stripes we are healed."

All of Isaiah 53 is about the substitution of Jesus for man. It says, "Surely he hath borne our griefs." *Young's Analytical Concordance to the Bible*[1] says *choli*, translated "griefs," means "sickness, weakness and pain." Surely He has borne *your* sickness, weakness and pain! Allow yourself to receive the magnitude of what God is speaking to you.

---

1. *Young's Analytical Concordance to the Bible*, Robert Young (Nashville: Thomas Nelson Publishers, 1980)

Jesus was smitten of God with sin and sickness in order for you to go free. Verse 6 tells us, "The Lord hath laid on him the iniquity of us all." Verse 10: "Yet it pleased the Lord to bruise him; he hath put him to grief...." (According to Dr. Young, the word *grief* means to "make sick" and should be translated, "He has made Him sick.")

According to the Word, what did Jesus do with your sickness? He bore it for you. It could not be God's will for you to be sick with the sickness that Jesus suffered for you.

Because God so loved the world, He engineered the substitution of His only begotten Son to redeem man from the curse of Satan.

"Christ hath redeemed us from the curse of the law, being made a curse for us: for it is written, Cursed is every one that hangeth on a tree" (Galatians 3:13).

Jesus was willing to take the curse in His own spirit, soul and body so that you would not have to continue under Satan's dominion.

There was no sickness before man became one with Satan. Sin is the root from which sickness came. As sin is the manifestation of spiritual death in the heart of man, sickness is the manifestation of spiritual death in the body of man.

Not only did Jesus pay the price for the new birth of your spirit and the healing of your body, He also bore the chastisement of your peace. Satan has no right to torment you mentally. You have been redeemed from fear, mental anxiety, depression or anything that keeps your mind from enjoying peace. You don't have to rely on Valium or any other tranquilizer. Jesus has already paid the price for you to be whole in your mind and enjoy peace. Do not allow Satan to steal your peace.

A Great Price

Jesus came to destroy the works of the devil—all of his works (1 John 3:8). He did not destroy sin only to leave sickness in dominion. Partial redemption from Satan's power would not have pleased God nor would it have fulfilled His plan for His family.

He redeemed the whole man—righteousness for his nature, peace for his mind and healing for his body. Redemption left nothing in force that came upon man because of sin. Jesus completely destroyed the works of the devil in the lives of men.

First Corinthians 6:20 says, "For ye are bought with a price." A great price! "Therefore glorify God in your body, and in your spirit, which are God's." There should not be any sickness in the Body of Christ. When one who is sick comes into our midst, the healing power of God should flow so that he receives healing.

In the book of Leviticus, Israel used a scapegoat.

The priest laid hands on a real goat, put the sins of the people on him and sent him to the wilderness—totally away from the people. That's what Jesus did with your sickness and disease! He bore them away from you! What you need to do is stand up in the Name of Jesus and command sickness and disease to go away from you. Give them no place in your body. Refuse to allow Satan to have any place in your body. Command sickness and disease to depart from your very presence—out of your home and your family.

The English language does not clearly communicate to us in the word "salvation" what the Greek word *sozo* really means. Train yourself to remember that salvation is not just the new birth of your spirit. It is also peace for your mind and healing for your body. *Vine's Expository Dictionary of Biblical Words*[2] says salvation denotes "deliverance, preservation; material and temporal deliverance from danger and apprehension."

Mark 16:15-16 says, "And he said unto them, Go ye into all the world, and preach the gospel to every creature. He that believeth and is baptized shall be saved; but he that believeth not shall be damned." The gospel is the good news of what Jesus did in His substitutionary sacrifice at the cross.

---

2. *Vine's Expository Dictionary of Biblical Words,* W.E. Vine (Thomas Nelson Publishers, 1985)

"By whose stripes ye were healed" is not a promise. It is a fact. It has already taken place. Jesus bore sickness away from you and by His stripes you were healed.

There is no sin so great that Jesus' sacrifice at Calvary will not cancel it and wipe it away—as though sin had never been.

The power of God cleanses and changes one who partakes of the gift of salvation until there is no trace of the old man or his sins. You become a new man, a new creature. Your new spirit is created in the righteousness of God.

There is no disease so devastating to the human body that the same sacrifice at Calvary will not cancel it and wipe it away, and heal that body as though sickness had never been!

The gospel is the good news of what Jesus did for every person in His substitutionary sacrifice at the cross. He bore your sins, so you do not have to bear them. You can be forgiven now! He did that for every sinner. He bore your diseases, so you do not have to bear them. You can be healed now! He did that for every sick man! He bore your pains. He did that for every sufferer. That is what the gospel is—good news of what Jesus did for all.

Jesus commanded that this good news be preached to every creature because everyone who hears it and believes it will be saved and healed now.

As the Body of Christ, we do not have to tolerate sickness any longer. We do not have to tolerate disease any longer. Jesus paid the price for our redemption from all the curse of the law. As an act of our will, we are the ones to set into motion the law of the Spirit of life in Christ Jesus.

Proclaim Your Redemption

Receive God's Word as words spoken to you by God Himself. It is His desire that you walk in this life in complete wholeness—spirit, soul and body. Proclaim your redemption from the works of Satan. Stop his maneuvers and operations against you in every area of life. He will flee from you as you apply the Word in faith, and sickness and disease will depart from your body! Allow the gospel, which is the power of God unto salvation, to work for you and deliver you from sickness, disease, grief, pain, fear and torment. This freedom belongs to you. Jesus has paid in full for you to be made whole—spirit, soul and body.

Evangelist T.L. Osborn says, "Any person can turn any promise of God into the power of God equal to what it promises, by believing that promise enough to act upon it." If you believe this gospel that I've shared with you, *now* is the time to act.

As you proclaim your freedom in Jesus' Name, give action to the Word that you have read.

If you are not born again, make Jesus Christ your Lord and Savior.

If you are paralyzed, move.

If you are deaf, hear.

If you are lame, leap up and walk.

If there is something that you could not do before, *do it now!*

Say this out loud with all boldness:

"The gospel that I have heard is the power of God unto salvation. I confess Jesus Christ as Lord over my life: spirit, soul and body. I receive the power of God to make me sound, whole, delivered, saved and healed. Now! I act on the Word of God and I receive the power of God.

"Sickness, disease, pain, I resist you in the Name of Jesus. You are not the will of God. I enforce the Word of God on you. I will not tolerate you in my life. Leave my presence. I will never allow you back. My days of sickness and disease are over! I am the healed. I am saved. The power of sickness has been forever broken over my life.

"Jesus bore my sickness, weakness and pain. And I am forever free. Sickness shall no longer lord it over me. Sin shall no longer lord it over me. Fear shall no longer lord it over me. Satan shall no longer lord it over me. I have been redeemed from the curse of the law. I proclaim my freedom in Jesus' Name.

"*Today* the gospel is the power of God to me unto salvation. I receive the gospel.

"I act on the gospel. I am made whole in Jesus' Name!"

Act! Praise. Move. See. Hear. Straighten up! Be delivered! Be free. Be sound. Be healed in the Name of Jesus!

Prayer for Salvation and Baptism in the Holy Spirit

Heavenly Father, I come to You in the Name of Jesus. Your Word says, "Whosoever shall call on the name of the Lord shall be saved" (Acts 2:21). I am calling on You. I pray and ask Jesus to come into my heart and be Lord over my life according to Romans 10:9-10: "If thou shalt confess with thy mouth the Lord Jesus, and shalt believe in thine heart that God hath raised him from the dead, thou shalt be saved. For with the heart man believeth unto righteousness; and with the mouth confession is made unto salvation." I do that now. I confess that Jesus is Lord, and I believe in my heart that God raised Him from the dead.

I am now reborn! I am a Christian—a child of Almighty God! I am saved! You also said in Your Word, "If ye then, being evil, know how to give good gifts unto your children: HOW MUCH MORE shall your heavenly Father give the Holy Spirit to them that ask him?" (Luke 11:13). I'm also asking You to fill me with the Holy Spirit. Holy Spirit, rise up within me as I praise God. I fully expect to speak with other tongues as You give me the utterance (Acts 2:4). In Jesus' Name. Amen!

Begin to praise God for filling you with the Holy Spirit. Speak those words and syllables you receive—not in your own language, but the language given to you by the Holy Spirit. You have to use your own voice. God will not force you to speak. Don't be concerned with how it sounds. It is a heavenly language!

Continue with the blessing God has given you and pray in the spirit every day.

You are a born-again, Spirit-filled believer. You'll never be the same!

Find a good church that boldly preaches God's Word and obeys it. Become part of a church family who will love and care for you as you love and care for them.

We need to be connected to each other. It increases our strength in God. It's God's plan for us.

Make it a habit to watch the *Believer's Voice of Victory* television broadcast and become a doer of the Word, who is blessed in his doing (James 1:22-25).

About the Author

Gloria Copeland is a noted author and minister of the gospel whose teaching ministry is known throughout the world. Believers worldwide know her through Believers' Conventions, Victory Campaigns, magazine articles, teaching audios and videos, and the daily and Sunday *Believer's Voice of Victory* television broadcast, which she hosts with her husband, Kenneth Copeland. She is known for Healing School, which she began teaching and hosting in 1979 at KCM meetings. Gloria delivers the Word of God and the keys to victorious Christian living to millions of people every year.

Gloria is author of the New York Times best-seller, *God's Master Plan for Your Life* and *Live Long, Finish Strong,* as well as numerous other favorites, including *God's Will for You, Walk With God, God's Will Is Prosperity, Hidden Treasures* and *To Know Him.* She has also co-authored several books with her husband, including *Family Promises, Healing Promises* and the best-selling daily devotionals, *From Faith to Faith* and *Pursuit of His Presence.*

She holds an honorary doctorate from Oral Roberts University. In 1994, Gloria was voted Christian Woman of the Year, an honor conferred on women whose example demonstrates outstanding Christian leadership. Gloria is also the co-founder and vice president of Kenneth Copeland Ministries in Fort Worth, Texas.

Learn more about Kenneth Copeland Ministries by visiting our website at **kcm.org**

Materials to Help You
Receive Your Healing
by Gloria Copeland

Books

* And Jesus Healed Them All
  God's Prescription for Divine Health
  God's Will for Your Healing
* Harvest of Health
  Words That Heal (gift book with CD enclosed)

Audio Resources
    Be Made Whole—Live Long, Live Healthy
    God Is a Good God
    God Wants You Well
    Healing Confessions (CD and minibook)
    Healing School

DVD Resources
    Be Made Whole—Live Long, Live Healthy
    Know Him As Healer

* Available in Spanish

When The LORD first spoke to Kenneth and Gloria Copeland about starting the *Believer's Voice of Victory* magazine...

He said: *This is your seed. Give it to everyone who ever responds to your ministry, and don't ever allow anyone to pay for a subscription!*

For nearly 40 years, it has been the joy of Kenneth Copeland Ministries to bring the good news to believers. Readers enjoy teaching from ministers who write from lives of living contact with God, and testimonies from believers experiencing victory through God's Word in their everyday lives.

Today, the *BVOV* magazine is mailed monthly, bringing encouragement and blessing to believers around the world. Many even use it as a ministry tool, passing it on to others who desire to know Jesus and grow in their faith!

Request your FREE subscription to the
***Believer's Voice of Victory* magazine today!**

Go to **freevictory.com** to subscribe online or, call us at
1-800-600-7395 (U.S. only) or **+1-817-852-6000**.

We're Here for You!®

Your growth in God's WORD and victory in Jesus are at the very center of our hearts. In every way God has equipped us, we will help you deal with the issues facing you, so you can be the **victorious overcomer** He has planned for you to be.

The mission of Kenneth Copeland Ministries is about all of us growing and going together. Our prayer is that you will take full advantage of all The LORD has given us to share with you.

Wherever you are in the world, you can watch the *Believer's Voice of Victory* broadcast on television (check your local listings), the Internet at kcm.org or on our digital Roku channel.

Our website, **kcm.org,** gives you access to every resource we've developed for your victory. And, you can find contact information for our international offices in Africa, Asia, Australia, Canada, Europe, Ukraine and our headquarters in the United States.

Each office is staffed with devoted men and women, ready to serve and pray with you. You can contact the worldwide office nearest you for assistance, and you can call us for prayer at our U.S. number, +1-817-852-6000, 24 hours every day!

We encourage you to connect with us often and let us be part of your everyday walk of faith!

Jesus Is LORD!

Kenneth & Gloria Copeland

Kenneth and Gloria Copeland